A TRUE BOOK™

Animals Helping with Healing

ANN O. SQUIRE

Children's Press®
An Imprint of Scholastic Inc.
New York Toronto London Auckland Sydney
Mexico City New Delhi Hong Kong
Danbury, Connecticut

Content Consultant
Dr. Stephen S. Ditchkoff
Professor of Wildlife Sciences
Auburn University
Auburn, Alabama

Library of Congress Cataloging-in-Publication Data
Squire, Ann, author.
 Animals helping with healing / by Ann O. Squire.
   pages cm. — (A true book)
 Summary: "Learn how animals can be trained to work in health care positions or used for therapy."—
Provided by publisher.
 Audience: Ages 9–12.
 Audience: Grades 4 to 6.
 Includes bibliographical references and index.
 ISBN 978-0-531-20508-2 (library binding) — ISBN 978-0-531-20534-1 (pbk.)
1. Animals—Therapeutic use—Juvenile literature. 2. Animals as aids for people with disabilities—
Juvenile literature. 3. Working animals—Juvenile literature. I. Title. II. Series: True book.
 RM931.A65S47 2015
 636.088'6—dc23   2014030572

© 2015 Scholastic Inc.
All rights reserved. Published in 2015 by Children's Press, an imprint of Scholastic Inc. Published
simultaneously in Canada. Printed in China 62
SCHOLASTIC, CHILDREN'S PRESS, A TRUE BOOK™, and associated logos are trademarks and/or
registered trademarks of Scholastic Inc.
1 2 3 4 5 6 7 8 9 10 R 24 23 22 21 20 19 18 17 16 15

**Front cover: A therapy dog
comforting a young girl**

**Back cover: Rojo the therapy llama
visiting patients in a hospital**

Find the Truth!

Everything you are about to read is true *except* for one of the sentences on this page.

Which one is **TRUE**?

T or F Trained dogs are 100 percent accurate at sniffing out peanuts, drugs, and bombs.

T or F Pigs, monkeys, horses, and many other animals can help in healing.

Find the answers in this book.

3

Contents

THE **BIG** TRUTH!

This rat helps humans with its great sense of smell.

4 Rats Helping Humans

5 Animal-Assisted Therapy

Many kinds of animals can participate in animal-assisted therapy.

Playing fetch with a dog is a great way for a person to relieve stress.

CHAPTER 1

Dogs Helping People

If you have pets, you know that spending time with them makes you feel good. When you have a bad day, there is nothing like playing a game of fetch with your dog or snuggling on the couch with your cat to lift your mood. Animals can cheer us up with their funny antics. They can make us feel loved. Sometimes they even seem to understand what we are thinking.

Spending time with an animal is more than just fun, it's good for you!

Daily walks provide exercise for both dogs and their owners.

Dogs can help their owners cope with stress and recover from diseases.

A Healthy Choice

We know animals make us feel good. But did you know that animals can actually help people be healthy? Researchers have found that people who have pets are less likely to suffer from heart disease. And among people who have heart attacks, dog owners are more likely to survive than those who do not have a dog.

Relaxing With Animals

Most dog owners walk their pets at least once each day. So it is possible that this extra exercise helps to keep these people healthier than those who are less active. But it's not just about exercise. Another study looked at people with high blood pressure and stressful jobs. Half of them adopted a dog or a cat, and the other half did not. After six months, the pet owners all had less stress and lower blood pressure.

Dogs can be very beneficial to workers with stressful jobs.

9

Diabetes Alert Dogs

Animals help us stay healthy just by interacting with us. And with special training, some animals can help people deal with **chronic** diseases. Odetta is a black Labrador retriever. Her owner, Kathy, has type 1 **diabetes**. Kathy must control the amount of sugar in her blood with injections of a substance called insulin. Exercise, stress, and other factors can cause a rapid drop in blood sugar for people with diabetes. This can cause dizziness, confusion, or even **seizures** and blackouts.

Diabetics must frequently inject themselves with insulin to prevent harmful symptoms.

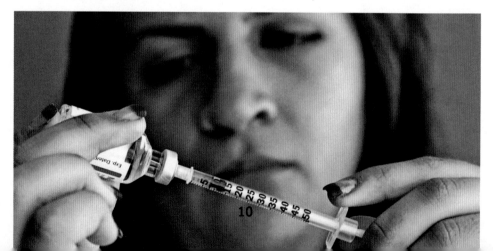

Diabetes alert dogs stay by their owners' sides at all times.

Many people with diabetes cannot tell when their blood sugar is getting too low. By the time they realize it is happening, the symptoms may be very severe. Odetta has been trained to sniff out changes in Kathy's blood. She can tell when her owner's blood sugar is dropping. When this happens, she alerts Kathy, even waking her up in the middle of the night if necessary. This gives Kathy a chance to treat her low blood sugar before her symptoms become serious.

Seizure Alert Dogs

Dogs also help people with **epilepsy,** a disorder of the nervous system that causes seizures. Some seizures are very mild, but others can be severe enough to cause unconsciousness. Some dogs show an ability to predict seizures. They warn their owners minutes or even hours in advance. How they are able to do this is still a mystery. Some people think the dogs detect a small change in the person's behavior or scent before the seizure starts.

Timeline

2001

A guide dog saves her owner's life by leading him out of the World Trade Center during the terrorist attacks of September 11, 2001.

1800s

Leeches become a common tool in the medical practice of bloodletting.

12

Not all dogs can predict seizures. However, they can help people with epilepsy in other ways. If the owner suffers a seizure, the dog can summon help. It might even be trained to press a button on the phone to call 911. Some epilepsy medicines can make it hard for people to keep their balance while walking. A dog can be trained to walk alongside its owner to provide stability. For patients who are afraid to be alone during a seizure, such as children, a dog can offer comfort and reassurance.

2005

A cat named Oscar is adopted by a nursing home in Rhode Island and begins predicting the deaths of patients.

2007

Two black Labradors named Budge and Boe travel to Iraq as the first therapy dogs to work in combat zones.

Dogs for Disabilities

For children with **autism**, a service dog can be a lifeline to the world. Many children with this condition have trouble communicating or forming relationships with other people. A service dog can be a quiet companion who comforts and protects the child. Sometimes autistic children who have never communicated with people will start talking to and playing with their dogs. From there, they often go on to form relationships with people.

A girl with autism poses next to her support dog, Merlin.

Allergy Dogs

Daily life can be challenging for people with severe allergies to peanuts, milk, or other common foods. Many foods contain very tiny amounts of these substances. The amounts are so small that people can't detect them. However, it is still enough to trigger an attack in someone who is allergic. Because of their sharp sense of smell, dogs can be trained to detect these hidden **allergens**. For example, a dog might alert its owner when it catches a whiff of peanuts. Allergen-detecting dogs can't catch everything, though. If the scent is too old or the food is in a container that blocks the odor, the dog might miss it.

Like service dogs, guide horses accompany their owners almost everywhere.

CHAPTER 2

Healing Horses

Dogs are popular companions and you may have seen guide dogs accompanying people who have trouble seeing or who are blind. But what about a guide horse? Just like guide dogs, miniature horses can be trained to lead their blind owners wherever they want to go. The miniature horses used for guide work are typically about the size and weight of a medium or large dog.

This miniature guide horse helps its visually impaired owner walk the city streets with ease.

Guide horses and their owners often form close bonds.

Horses typically live for 30 to 40 years.

Why Choose a Horse?

Why would someone want a guide horse instead of a guide dog? There are several reasons. A horse can be a better option for people with allergies or those who are afraid of dogs. Horses also have much longer life spans than dogs. They are very calm and strong, and they have excellent vision. Guide horses usually live outdoors when they are not working, so they are perfect for people who don't want a service animal with them all the time.

Therapy Horses

For men and women returning from war zones, adjusting to life at home can be a challenge. Many combat veterans have suffered brain injuries or **post-traumatic stress disorder** (PTSD). This can leave them anxious, depressed, and unable to cope with day-to-day life. Frustrated by their conditions, some veterans turn to alcohol or drugs. Others may become violent toward themselves or others.

Fighting in a war is extremely stressful.

Building Trust

Doctors have different ideas about the best ways to treat soldiers with PTSD. One approach that has been very successful is called equine-assisted psychotherapy. This treatment uses horses as therapists. Each veteran is paired up with a horse. He or she is assigned tasks such as learning to groom, care for, and eventually ride the horse. Throughout this process, the veteran and horse develop a relationship of friendship and trust.

A person may be helped through PTSD by taking care of and interacting with a horse.

Army soldiers guide a veteran as she rides a therapy horse.

Riding, grooming, and caring for horses are all part of equine-assisted therapy.

How Horses Help

Horses are **prey** animals, so they are always on the alert. In order to work with them, a person must use a calm and caring approach. If the person is angry or agitated, the horse will sense it and refuse to cooperate. Patients learn that they must remain calm in order to succeed. Eventually, they begin to feel calmer in their daily lives.

Leeches in Medicine

While it might seem a lot different from dogs, horses, or monkeys, the lowly leech has been used since ancient times to help patients heal. Leeches are spineless, wormlike animals that are typically found in freshwater environments such as lakes. They feed by attaching themselves to another animal, biting through the skin, and sucking the animal's blood.

Sounds harmful, doesn't it? You might wonder how leeches could help anyone, let alone a sick person. The answer lies in the creature's saliva. It contains a substance that prevents blood from clotting. It also contains an anesthetic, which relieves pain. Doctors use leeches for transplant surgeries, skin grafts, and the reattachment of body parts. In these situations, blood clots can prevent healing. The leech's saliva helps blood flow freely, speeding up the healing process.

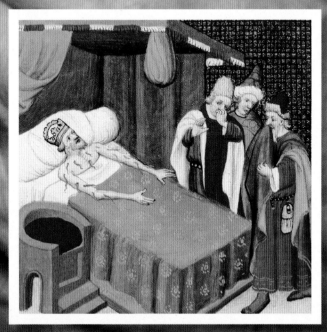

Monkeys can use their hands to do almost anything a human can do.

CHAPTER 3

Monkey Helpers

In addition to service dogs and horses, monkeys can also help their human companions. Some tasks such as turning on a light, changing a TV channel, retrieving dropped objects, or turning the pages in a book can be difficult or impossible for people who are confined to wheelchairs or cannot use their arms or legs. In these situations, a monkey helper can be the ideal solution.

Their intelligence and ability to learn complex tasks make monkeys perfect helpers for disabled people.

Capuchins are native to South and Central America.

Capuchin monkeys trained as helpers are born in captivity, and not taken from the wild.

The Perfect Helper

Capuchin monkeys are small and agile. They are among the most intelligent of **primates**. They also have long life spans, living up to about 40 years. These qualities make them perfect as helpers for disabled people. It takes a lot of time and training for a monkey to become a service animal. In fact, training doesn't even begin until the monkey is about 10 years old.

Learning to Live With People

For the first years of its life, each monkey lives with a foster family. There, it learns to socialize with people in a home environment. The monkey gets used to interacting with pets, children, and other family members. It also becomes accustomed to the sights, sounds, and smells of a typical home. Once the monkey has matured, it's time for it to begin training.

The first step in training a monkey is helping it become comfortable around people.

Going to Monkey College

Each monkey progresses through the training program at its own pace. At the beginning, the monkey learns to associate the sound of a bell and words of praise with a tasty food reward. Next, the trainer shines a laser pointer on an object. When the monkey picks up or touches the object, it is rewarded with a treat. Eventually the bells are phased out, and the monkey learns to respond to just spoken praise.

A laser pointer is used to show a monkey where the On/Off button is located on a printer.

28

A trained monkey can open a CD player, insert a disc, and press play.

Graduation Day

During training, each monkey learns increasingly complicated tasks. By the time it graduates, the monkey can perform multistep jobs such as putting a water bottle in a holder, unscrewing the top, and inserting a straw. It can also operate CD and DVD players and other types of technology. After graduation, the monkey is ready to be placed with a disabled person who needs its help.

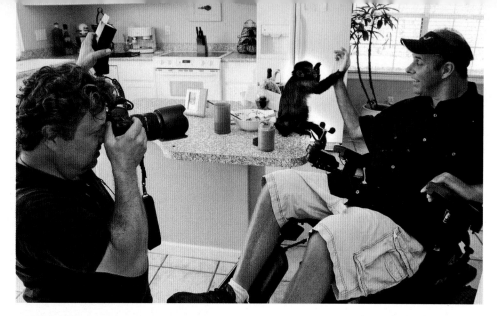

Minnie gives Craig a high five.

Craig and Minnie

Craig enjoyed sports and all kinds of activities until a serious car accident changed his life forever. A broken neck left him **paralyzed** from the shoulders down. Upset about his new limitations, Craig became depressed and lonely. Then his helper monkey, Minnie, came into his life. Minnie is able to get Craig a snack, find a book or magazine, and retrieve the phone if Craig drops it. But that's not all she does.

Craig says that the greatest thing about having Minnie around is the companionship she offers. Being responsible for Minnie's care has helped Craig to focus on her, rather than on his disability. With Minnie's help, he is able to be more independent. He is no longer nervous about living alone. Minnie is more than just Craig's helper. She is his best friend.

Minnie adjusts Craig's foot to make sure it stays on the footrest of the wheelchair.

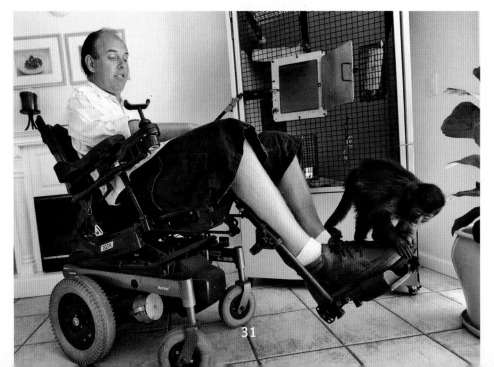

31

A doctor in Rwanda explains the TB treatment process to a sick patient.

CHAPTER 4

Rats Helping Humans

Rats are famous for spreading diseases. It might be hard to imagine they could possibly help people stay healthy. But specially trained rats in Africa are doing just that. They work to identify patients infected with tuberculosis (TB). TB is an infection that usually targets a person's lungs. Without proper treatment, TB can be fatal. In addition, infected people can spread the sickness by simply coughing or sneezing.

← TB kills an average of 5,000 people every day.

Detecting Deadly Diseases

TB is an especially serious threat in Africa. In the country of Tanzania, it is the third-leading cause of death. The key to controlling the spread of TB is quick identification and treatment of people who are infected. The traditional way of checking for TB is for a lab technician to look at samples of thick liquids from the lungs under a microscope. Unfortunately, this method has drawbacks.

TB patients in Tanzania wait to receive medication.

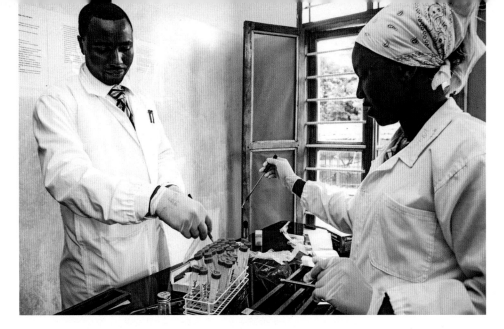
Lab technicians test samples for TB.

In Tanzania, a lab technician can analyze only about 40 samples per day. This is not nearly enough to keep up with all the potential TB cases that come in. Additionally, fewer than half of the samples are correctly identified. As a result, many patients are sent back home unknowingly carrying the disease. Without treatment, they become sicker and may also spread the infection to others. But a nonprofit group called APOPO is trying to change the situation with the help of African giant pouched rats.

An African giant pouched rat's strong sense of smell and ability to learn quickly make it perfect for helping to detect TB.

Sniffing Out Tuberculosis

Like all rodents, African giant pouched rats have a terrific sense of smell. They are trained by APOPO workers who first teach the rats to associate the sound of a clicker with a food reward. Next, the rats are given positive and negative TB samples to smell. When they sniff a container holding a positive sample, the trainer sounds the clicker and gives the rat a treat.

Finding False Negatives

As training progresses, the rats learn to pick out positive samples from many possible containers. A fully trained rat can screen 100 or more samples in 15 to 20 minutes. This task would take a human lab technician more than two full days! The rats are not only faster but also more accurate than their human counterparts. They are even able to pick out positive samples that humans have judged to be negative.

A lab technician observes as a rat sniffs samples.

A resident at the
Thompson House gets
a holiday greeting
from Zena, a 4-year-old
miniature dachshund.

CHAPTER 5

Animal-Assisted Therapy

For people in nursing homes, hospitals, or other medical facilities, day-to-day life can become boring and routine. In some cases, family members and friends no longer visit. People can begin to lose touch with the outside world. For these people, animal-assisted therapy (also known as pet therapy) can improve their lives and moods.

Therapy animals can bring joy to people who are ill or nearing the end of their lives.

Visiting Friends

Trained therapy dogs pay regular visits to the residents of these institutions. Patients undergoing difficult medical procedures, people in nursing homes, and abused children have all been helped by therapy animals. A sense of calm and a decrease in stress are two of the biggest benefits of spending time with a therapy dog.

A visit from a dog can help pick up almost anyone's spirits.

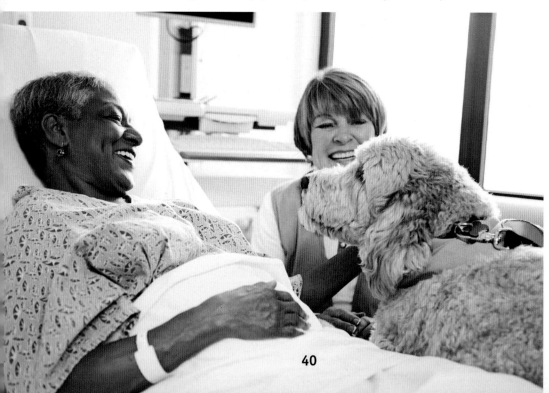

A therapy dog visits mourners at a memorial to the victims of the Sandy Hook shootings.

Healing Trauma

Therapy animals can bring companionship and comfort to people who have experienced traumatic events. After the 2012 shootings at Sandy Hook Elementary School in Newtown, Connecticut, a therapy dog named Spartacus spent several months at the school. Spartacus offered comfort to teachers and students. He and other therapy animals made such a big difference that the state of Connecticut passed a law making therapy animals an official part of its plans for dealing with disasters.

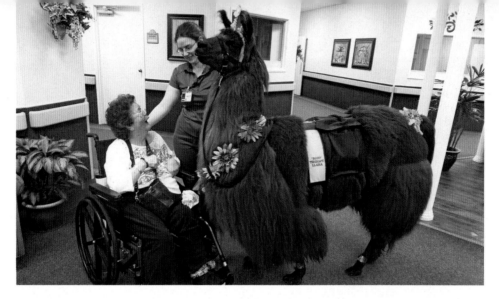

While llamas and alpacas are less common than other types of therapy animals, they are just as good at helping people feel better.

Not Just Dogs

Cats, rabbits, guinea pigs, and many other animals can work as animal therapists. Buttercup is a miniature pot-bellied pig who visits special-needs students in San Francisco, California, schools. He helps autistic children improve their social skills. Rojo, a llama, and Napoleon, an alpaca, are registered therapy animals in Vancouver, Washington. They regularly visit hospitals and schools to surprise and delight the residents.

A Very Unusual Cat

Oscar the therapy cat has spent his life at a nursing home in Rhode Island, after being adopted as a kitten. Unlike many therapy animals, Oscar doesn't spend a lot of time with the patients. He would rather look out the window or walk up and down the hall. That changes, however, when a patient is near death. Oscar seems to know when a patient has only a few hours to live. He curls up on the person's bed and stays with him or her until the end. Over the years, he has correctly predicted the deaths of at least 50 patients. No one knows how he does it. ★

Number of TB sniffer rats trained so far in Tanzania: 54

Number of wrongly identified TB patients correctly diagnosed by TB sniffer rats in recent years: 3,000

Time required to train a sniffer rat: 9 months

Time required to train a capuchin helper monkey: 3 to 5 years

Number of smell receptors in a dog's nose: Around 300 million

Number of smell receptors in a human's nose: Around 6 million

Number of people in the United States suffering from type 1 diabetes: Around 3 million

Number of diabetes alert dogs working in the United States today: Several hundred

Did you find the truth?

(F) Trained dogs are 100 percent accurate at sniffing out peanuts, drugs, and bombs.

(T) Pigs, monkeys, horses, and many other animals can help in healing.

Resources

Books

Hansen, Rosanna. *Panda: A Guide Horse for Ann*. Honesdale, PA: Boyds Mills Press, 2005.

Rogers, Ellen. *Kasey to the Rescue: The Remarkable Story of a Monkey and a Miracle*. New York: Hyperion, 2010.

Tagliaferro, Linda. *Service Dogs*. New York: Bearport Publishing, 2005.

Visit this Scholastic Web site for more information on animals helping with healing:

★ www.factsfornow.scholastic.com

Enter the keywords **Animals Helping With Healing**

Important Words

allergens (AL-ur-jenz) — substances that cause people to have allergic reactions

autism (AW-tiz-uhm) — a condition that causes someone to have trouble learning, communicating, and forming relationships with people

chronic (KRAH-nik) — lasting for a long time or returning periodically

diabetes (dye-uh-BEE-teez) — a disease in which there is too much sugar in the blood

epilepsy (EP-uh-lep-see) — a disease of the brain that may cause a person to have sudden blackouts or to lose control of his or her movements

paralyzed (PAR-uh-lyzd) — unable to move or feel part of the body

post-traumatic stress disorder (POHST-truh-MAT-ik STREHS dis-OR-dur) — also called PTSD; a psychiatric disorder that can occur after experiencing or witnessing life-threatening events such as military combat

prey (PRAY) — an animal that is hunted by another animal for food

primates (PRYE-mates) — members of the group of mammals that includes monkeys, apes, and humans

seizures (SEE-zhurz) — sudden attacks or spasms

Index

Page numbers in **bold** indicate illustrations.

About the Author

Ann O. Squire is a psychologist and an animal behaviorist. Before becoming a writer, she studied the behavior of rats, tropical fish in the Caribbean, and electric fish from central Africa. Her favorite part of being a writer is the chance to learn as much as she can about all sorts of topics. In addition to the Animal Helpers books, Dr. Squire has written about many different animals, from lemmings to leopards and cicadas to cheetahs. She lives in Long Island City, New York.

PHOTOGRAPHS ©: age fotostock/F Volk: 22 background, 23 background; AP Images: 12 right (Chao Soi Cheong), 15 (Jessica Hill), 19 (Jim MacMillan), 18 (Michael Kinney, The Altus Times), 20 (Mike Cardew, Akron Beacon Journal), 14 (Press Association), 10 (Reed Saxon), 30 (Richard Vogel), 11 (Scott Mason, The Winchester Star), 16 (Steven Senne), 13, 43 (Stew Milne); APOPO: 37; Bridgeman Art Library/Bibliotheque Nationale, Paris, France/Archives Charmet: 3 inset, 12 left; Getty Images: 21 (Chris Hondros), 32 (David Evans/National Geographic), 27, 44 (Susan Biddle/The Washington Post); Helping Hands/Kathleen Duncan: 28; Landov: 34 (Emmanuel Kwitema/Reuters), 4, 29 (Jim Bourg/Reuters), 41 (Mike Segar/Reuters); Maarten Boersema/www.boersemabeeldtaal.nl: 35; Media Bakery: 9 (Laura Doss), cover, 8; Mtn Peaks Therapy Llamas & Alpacas: back cover, 5 bottom, 42; Newscom/Paul Rodriguez/Zuma Press: 31; Redux/David Butow: 24; Reuters/Sala Lewis: 5 top, 36; Shutterstock, Inc.: 6 (Eldad Carin), cover background (herjua), 26 (LeonP), 3, 40 (Monkey Business Images); The Image Works/Kathy McLaughlin: 38.